MW01002334

◇◇◇◇◇◇◇◇◇

WINTER SOLSTICE

◇◇◇◇◇◇◇◇◇

WINTER SOLSTICE

AN ESSAY

Nina MacLaughlin

BLACK SPARROW PRESS

BOSTON

Published in 2023 by BLACK SPARROW PRESS

GODINE
Boston, Massachusetts
godine.com

This essay originally appeared in a different form on *The Paris Review Daily.*

LIBRARY OF CONGRESS CATALOGING-IN-PUBLICATION DATA
Names: MacLaughlin, Nina, author.
Title: Winter solstice : an essay / Nina MacLaughlin.
Description: Boston : Black Sparrow Press, 2023.
Identifiers: LCCN 2023006879 (print) | LCCN 2023006880
  (ebook) | ISBN 9781574232578 (paperback) | ISBN
  9781574232585 (ebook)
Subjects: LCSH: Winter solstice. | Winter. | LCGFT: Essays.
Classification: LCC PS3613.A27358 W56 2023 (print) | LCC
  PS3613.A27358 (ebook) | DDC 814/.6--dc23/eng/20230222
LC record available at https://lccn.loc.gov/2023006879
LC ebook record available at https://lccn.loc.gov/2023006880

SECOND PRINTING, 2023
Printed in The United States of America

Contents

Inhale the Darkness

Two boys strung the lights on houses in Ohio. On weekends into winter, the work put money in their pockets as they moved around the neighborhoods. When nighttime arrived in the afternoon, they climbed their ladders. One held the loop and fed the cord to the other who reached and fastened, line of lights between them. Some bulbs were sharp and thorny, other strands had round fat egg drops. Some icy white, some a warmer glowing gold, some the mix of red, orange, blue, and green, blinking through the night on the smalltown streets. They strung bulbs under gutters, rimmed front porches, edged the roofline trim. They raised their ladders to the peaks and made huge arrow tips of light aimed into the big black nightsky. They helixed little lights around lampposts, and they passed the strings of light round and round the oak tree, the holly bush, the evergreen, so it looked as though the constellations themselves had been blown by wind and caught in the net of branches. They breathed in pine needle, branches caught the collars of their coats, pitch stickied the tips of their workgloves. When they finished a job, they knocked on the door, brought the family out into the cold, ready?, and they flipped the switch, ta-da!, and the kids leapt and cheered and turned around at their parents, eyes glittering, to see if they saw, too. And the parents made a sound, of joy or relief, with a firework glow on their faces like summer. But it wasn't summer, and the boys saw their breath as they worked, lighting up the darkness.

It's an old impulse. To honor the dark with festivals of light, to battle it with same. Days are getting darker as we hurtle into winter, it comes at us faster every year. I am listening to sycamore leaves rustle down the sidewalk in front of my apartment. It's somewhere in the forties. The wind is strong. Its voice changes this time of year, as though coming from darker lungs, and the leaves are at their loudest, last rattle before long quiet. In his fevered novel *Malicroix*, Henri Bosco describes this almost-winter moment of the year, "when the world was poised on a pure ridge," balanced between two seasons, casting "a glance back at the aging autumn, still misty with its wild moods, to contemplate deadly winter from afar." The misty mood is behind us. We're looking now at something dark and wilder.

The river I live near turns black in November. It bristles against this wind, white fur rising on the backs of fast black animals. On a recent midday I stood on its banks, first snow—early—of the season, the river black and the fat flakes fell and the sky was the thick almost-white of the sky when it snows, which is one of my favorite things of being alive, seeing the sky almost-white when it snows. The fat flakes fell into the black river and became river. The air felt clean and bright in the lungs. From the west, a pair of swans appeared, flying low above the river, through the snow, white above black, white against almost-white, and close enough to hear the thwap of their wide wings against the air and a guttural croaking from their throats, more amphibious than avian. All went still as they flew by, everything quieted inside, the special stillness of an unexpected encounter, then a churn of associations—the swan's position in alchemy as an initial confrontation with the soul; Leda and a swan-beak speculum; the ten-starred constellation Cygnus caught glittering in galactic branches.

It was a secret Friday ritual, to meet along the riverbank at noon and drink two beers and talk and laugh and then go home and fuck with wildness in our eyes and all the demons there. We watched those swans, cans held in our cold hands. Our breath plumed from the hot inside. Dark and light, warmth and cold, underworld and Eden. No one without the other, when it comes to the major forces in this world. "That first white cloud of escaping breath is proof that we are alive," writes Han Kang in her wintery *The White Book*. "Cold air rushes into dark lungs, soaks up the heat of our body, and is exhaled as perceptible form." Out of the darkness perceptible form, great white birds of breath.

Dark makes its annual inhale of light. It seems night all the time now, and it'll keep getting nighter as we spin toward the solstice. If you follow the meteorological calendar, December 1 is the first day of winter. If you follow the astrological calendar, calibrated by the position of the sun, winter begins on the 21st or 22nd of December when the earth, in the Northern Hemisphere, is tilted farthest away from the sun, when we're delivered the longest night of the year. These are lampposts to string your lights around, ways of managing your time, systems to agree with and believe in.

What's the start of the season for you? Is it: the first time you see your breath; the first potato-chip crisp of ice on a puddle; the first snow; the first mug of hot chocolate; tinsel; menorah; mistletoe? Is it: when the river freezes; when you hear a Christmas carol in CVS; when you lower the storm windows; see a wreath on a neighbor's door; a candy cane; a persimmon; a pomegranate; eggnog in the dairy aisle; scarf around your throat; a certain pair of socks; the changed quality of blaze in sunset sky? Is it a creeping spider of malaise? A vague and frightening fuzz-edged feeling of hopelessness when the sun starts to sink too soon, a bottom giving way beneath you? A shadow at the back of the brain that, if you find yourself in too quiet a moment, gives an electric sizzle of static you can almost hear? A snarled black nest of fear in your chest and the upped urge to have another drink? The first fire? The first frost?

Loss is in the air. Summer's juicy verdure gives way to something husked and brittle. The colors dull, the plants fuzz, release last seed, go black. There's something cruel about it. On a plane some years ago, the stranger strapped in next to me talked about winter in Chicago. "You never been to Chicago in winter?" he said. "I've never been to Chicago," I said. "Well we got a wind so cold we call it the Hawk," he said. It sounded like a mean thing.

Heat slips off, chased by the hawk, and the smolder has to come from within. Winter makes us know the hollows. Darkness creeps in from both sides and pushes us to that pure ridge, all the way exposed. Peer over. Scope the abyss. The fear is ancient and uncomplicated, part of our human-animal inheritance, the surging fury of survival: will I be warm enough, will I have enough to eat, will the cold air reach my bones, will it keep getting darker, will the darkness swallow me, will it swallow us all together? Will I see the spring?

The gape feels wider now, the fear pulsing at a different frequency. The losses—individual, collective, major and minor, the way we move through our days, the way we ache and dream—are too many and too grave to list. Maybe you have felt this, too, involved in whatever moment of your day, a trip to the pharmacy, a walk after dinner, folding the laundry on the bed, when a sense, new, overtakes you, that something has collected above us, that grief itself has become a thin layer of the atmosphere, its particles collecting in the overlap between troposphere and stratosphere, particulates of grief surrounding the whole globe. I feel this sometimes now. From October through December, the polar night jet, a stratospheric westerly wind, gets stronger, swirling around the polar vortex, gusting the cold air into our winters, and it stirs this salted fog of grief that's collected over these last years. We breathe it in, it gets caught in our hair, it settles on us as we sleep.

"In a world of facts, death is merely one more fact," writes the poet Octavio Paz. And we lump it in with the rest: the full moon in December is the Long Night Moon; each tiny bulb lighting up the porch rail or the front-yard bush uses .5 watts of energy; foxes do not hibernate; more people are born in August—that is, conceived in December—than any other month, this long night heat, the fear that pulls us close; six liters is the average lung capacity for a male, four point two for a female, inhale, take the coming winter into you; the stars know where they belong, and the moon, and the sun; just because you can't see clouds of breath in spring or summer or fall does not mean those clouds do not exist, we walk through what came from inside each other, we breathe each other in; the places where the creatures sleep away the winter are called hibernacula, sweet dreams, creatures; the wind does not dream but it brings dreams; you, I, they, brothers, sisters, parents, pals, children, strangers, loves, god bless us every one, all will not be anymore. Last month the leaves on the birch tree across the street turned gold. It started at the edges of the leaves, gold around the rims, and gold took over green as the month went on. Archeologists have been finding mummies with tongues of gold, all the better to communicate with Osiris, god of the underworld. A gold-dipped tongue speaks the language of time. One more fact in a world of facts.

What's death in a world of stories?

In a world of stories, maybe a door exists that opens to the possibility that the ending's not always the same. In a world of stories, maybe death is all potential, another means of moving on. And on we go, absorbed into the wet warm belly of eternity, or the roaring big black void, back here as a robin or a wren, in dusted orbit around another planet's moon, riding on the light.

For now, here we are. Confused and frightened, angry maybe, too, but that's just the fear again. A little mixed up about where we are, dangling between two eternities like a drop about to fall from the faucet. My sweater's warm and the kitchen's warm, with that amber warmth that comes when there's a soup on the stove in the early evening, the sky the jewelly blue before it hardens into dark, steam collecting on the windowpanes so it fogs the glass and makes it harder to see the darkness pressing in. But it does press in. There's wine on the counter and glasses on the shelf. A glittering on the inside of the chest—it's fear—and the hotter, deeper smolder below, that's something else, and these long winter nights acquaint me with it.

The opposites are right now in tension, twinned and twined, the great cosmic tug. And the tug is never stronger than in this moment, as we sink into the deepest part of darkness. A bashing against, a blurring with, a pulling away, and a drawing in. Khaos emerged at the birth of the universe, preceding the rest of the primeval gods. A state of disordered darkness, a void where nothing was named. Her name meant gap, chasm, yawn. Absence. Form was exhaled from the lung of that darkness. Right now, the darkness takes a deep breath in. Hold tight. We're riding the backs of the swans. There's no flying without land, no emptiness without an edge. The boundaries begin to dissolve. And yet:

Here you are.

Here you are, the winter tells us.

An offer and a fact.

The Shadows Below the Shadows

DECEMBER AND Demeter is grieving again, in this world of stories and facts. Her daughter, Persephone, full of grace, with dark eyebrows and thick hair, picked violets, hyacinths, and white lilies in the field in the sun. To see her was to feel the word *cusp*. Cusp! One of the sexiest words for the swell it promises, all its verge and volume. Hades, lord of the underworld, cracked the earth and snatched her, cold dry hand around the soft flesh of her belly. He tugged her down to the underworld to be his unconsenting bride. *The flowers,* Persephone thought as she plunged. She'd dropped the violets, the hyacinths, the lilies, and the flowers fell into the fracture, too, lost their color, curled into themselves, crumbled into dust.

It happened so fast! From flower picking in the sun to being queen in the land of the dead. It smells like ash in the underworld, like coffee grounds at the bottom of the bin, like nickels and plant rot and smoke. The breath of excess, the weary all-wrong breath of someone who saw too much the night before. All the surfaces are cold and the curtains-closed light gives every shadow a secret. Persephone grew wan in the gloom. Aboveground, Demeter closed growth. In a grieving fury, she ripped the quilt of comfort and warmth and bounty off the surface of the earth. Wilt, starvation, cold. No fruit, no crop, no fat goats whose throats to slit in sacrifice.

I planted a small garden in the spring. Zinnias, arugula, eggplant, tomatoes, and marigolds to keep the beetles away. Rich smell of soil and grassy scent of potential. Later, the taut dark eggplant skin shone in the sun. I pulled the sweet tomatoes from the vines, some whose skin had split, the push of pulpy flesh from within too much to bear. Still later, the wind changed, the sun retreated. I found an eggplant shriveled like an old woman's breast. The proud tomato plants slumped in their stands. A frost turned the green blood black. Harvest time had ended.

Zeus sent Hermes to the underworld to get Demeter's daughter back. Persephone leapt to her feet when he arrived. But Hades's gardener hissed from the shadows. Ascalaphus, the orchard minder, knew what she had done, and said so, rotten tattler. If you eat the food of the dead, you stay, and Persephone had swallowed six pomegranate seeds. The gardener held the forbidden fruit in his hand and the fuchsia juice slipped down the private part of his wrist. Each seed, one month under. She's down there now. And we're up here, buttoning our coats, eating carbohydrates, trying to remember to unclench our jaws.

There's something about the below, the magnetic tug of the dark. Let's see how dark it gets, let's see what's down there, a little lower, a little deeper, what's going to get revealed? I have a friend who likes to press a knife-blade to his wrist. "It makes me shiver," he says. "I feel it in all my tips." I wouldn't call him crazy. He's interested in the edge. "The descent to the Underworld is easy," Virgil cautions in *The Aeneid*. "But to retrace your steps, to climb back to the upper air— / there the struggle, there the labor lies." Sink down, not a problem. Return? No guarantees.

In Ireland, thirty miles north of Dublin near the River Boyne, there's a mound of earth with an opening. You can enter. A tight passageway leads to a chamber. A tomb at one time: human bones were found there, and long-gone chiselers carved triskelion, those ancient-art triple spirals, into certain stones. The passageway extends sixty feet, almost the length of two telephone poles, and at sunrise on the winter solstice, a shaft of sunlight enters through an opening above the entrance of the passageway. The beam travels down the tunnel and penetrates the chamber, spraying light into the deep dim basin. The place is called Newgrange, and it was built in 3200 BC. It is older, by hundreds of years, than Stonehenge and the Pyramids at Giza.

I entered a long time ago. It wasn't on the solstice, but they shine a light that mimics the way the sunbeam seeks the chamber on the darkest day of the year. The hush was total, we were all the way within, and the shaft slid past our bodies in silence and lit the deepest part of the tomb, the womb, the undermound, otherworld, and the megalithic spirals revolved across millennia. If you are someone who feels ghosts, or time, or the presence of deep-dead stone movers, peat farmers, priestesses, priests, bog queens, salmon kings, ubiquitous shapeshifters, you might feel them here. The souls who touched with their human hands the stones we stood below, the souls who tracked the sun and built a mound for it to enter, they made themselves present that day. In the hush, in the ancient charge of the chamber, in the light that came from high above and was welcomed deep below. I felt it in the shivery-heated feeling in my blood as we stood witnessing the silent coupling of sun god and earth goddess. They knew the angles, of earth and sun, of light and hope, five thousand years ago.

The whole earth spins tilted on its axis at 23.5 degrees. That tilt delivers us our seasons and it slants us now away from the sun and into winter. A seasonal and celestial paradox: we're closer to the sun in winter than we are in summer. It's not like lowering your palm toward a candle flame. The midday sun rides low during these solstice-close days. Low above the trees and the sea, low between the hills on the outskirts of town. The arc the sun describes has been flattening since its high peak on the summer solstice six months ago. Stand outside at midday in this short-day time of year, you'll see your shadow at its longest, darkness stretching out from under you over the surface of the earth, reaching for something and inviting you to follow. Our shadows achieve their great height these days; they come into their power. The earth right now is moving closer to the sun, and spinning faster as it does. It's so strange to think about, how fast the earth is spinning around the sun, nineteen miles per second, and picking up speed. Between the summer solstice and the winter solstice, in the small northeastern city where I live, we lose six hours and twelve minutes of daylight. Said otherwise: we gain those hours in darkness. We stand on the earth looking up and the stars burn brighter in winter—cold air can't hold moisture as well as warm air can, and moisture obscures the view. All the better to see Orion, Cetus, Ursa Major, Perseus. On the winter solstice, the sun at noon is directly over the Tropic of Capricorn, which runs at 23.5 degrees south of the equator.

Capricorn, that stomping, large-horned sea goat. Is there an earthier beast than the goat? They dance on rockfaces. Their cloven hooves leave ash prints on soft earth. They grunt, hum, holler with the voice of man. And I felt a funny mix of alarm and delight the first time I looked one in the eye and saw its pupils were rectangular. A raw gray early winter afternoon well into my adulthood at a farm on a hill in south central Connecticut, I paid a quarter for a pack of stale wafers in a wax paper pouch to feed the three goats penned to the left of the farm-stand shed. I pressed the wafer through the fence, the goat took it on its tongue, and I saw what I had not seen before. Goats with right-angled bands across the globes of their ice or amber colored eyes.

In a backyard after, a mile down the hill from the farm, someone's father said that the local news had broadcasted alerts of black bear sightings in the neighborhood. We stood by the pool, its turquoise tarp pulled taut, redbrown leaves shifting quick across its surface, moving from a small heap where they'd collected in the center. From the forest, from a place we couldn't see, an animal noise, a flat and nasal bleat. "What the fuck?" said the father. My mind didn't fill the darkening woods with a lumbering ursine mass. Hooves not paws. Another bleat. The farm, in summer, sells strawberries, tomatoes, honey, corn. The goats are there all winter, their coats thickening against the cold. Had one escaped? Rogue goat in the woods? The smell of soot, a crunch of twig, a colder wind against our necks, and somewhere unseen but close, two glittering watchful eyes, rectangular surveillance in the dimming space between the trees. Shouldn't the bears be sleeping? Shouldn't the goat be in its pen?

In Central Europe, a folklore lives in the figure of Krampus, a stomping satyr-like creature, furred animal from the waist down, furred man-goat from the waist up, with a pointed lashing long tongue and sharp fangs and great goat horns. The smell of woods and soot about him, dead-leaf tang of dark dens, half-intoxicating half-repugnant ungulate musk. His fur, not a thick-matted hay-coarse mess, but angel-hair lush, cashmerey. I might want to sink my fingers in it. He emerges this time of year as dark twin to the twinkle-eyed benevolence of old Saint Nick. His night, Krampusnacht, takes place on December 5. He carries a birch switch to whip the misbehavers, and the sack or basket slung over his shoulder bears no gifts: bad children get stuffed there. He knots the sack and drops them into a river like a squirming litter of unwanted kittens. That, or he eats them.

A way to motivate children to behave, sure, a fearful threat. You better watch out, you better not pout, et cetera. Stop tugging your sister's pigtails or Krampus will take you. Stop chasing the chickens or you'll get jammed in Kramp's sack. Be good, be right, behave, or Krampus will whisk you away forever. Motivation, and also, maybe, secret wish? A fantasy? Or perhaps this goat-horned punisher is the creatured embodiment of winter's danger. It's not just a chubby chuckling red-suited do-gooder in a flying sleigh who giveth but a furred fanged earthbound mischief maker who taketh away. Here we are, back to forces of dark and light.

Fleshing the shadows is one way to know the shadows better. When fears get faced and named, aren't they easier to encounter? When they come creeping, slithering, spidering in, as they always inevitably will, it's better, no?, to see a familiar silhouette, a recognizable cut of the jaw, that same tongue, that same staticky charge, those wild otherworldly eyes, you again, we've met before. Still unpleasant, still frightening, but at least it slots into a taxonomy of the monstrous. It's the formless unfamiliar, the shadow that lives below the shadow, the one we sense but have not named or cannot yet name, there's where the real terror lives. And so we name our monsters. Perhaps the pull of the dark is the urge to introduce ourselves to the shadows below the shadows. Come in, come in, let me know you better, let me look upon you, I have never seen the like of you before. Maybe they all have something to offer. After all, wouldn't we all like to live deliciously?

Saturn rules Capricorn, and Saturnalia was the ancient Roman festival honoring him, he a child-eater himself, a scythe-holding god of the agricultural cycles. The festival took place over seven days around the winter solstice. Feasts, gifts, mischief, the rules gave way, the chains of discipline were lifted. In this kind of boundary-dissolving extendo-fest, "we throw down our burdens of time and reason," writes Octavio Paz. Time dissolves; roles reverse; people drop into a simultaneous backward and forward. Reason gives way to something more bodily, blood-level, in a "sudden immersion in the formless, in pure being." Ecstasy, in other words. Kerry Howley writes of "ecstatic spectacle." History is full of it:

> If you were a fourteenth-century Latvian looking to leave yourself, you might mask up and dance through the streets reveling in Rabelaisian wonder . . . were you a nineteenth-century Paiute Indian in the American West, you might try your hand at ritual millenarian dance . . . or an ancient maenad, join the other womenfolk in ripping apart a live goat in the Greek countryside.

In rare moments, we dissolve and pass formless through the membrane into a shimmering of raw perception, into union with the All. There is no knowing or thinking there. A period of rupture, of release, of the wholest and full-bodiest attention, every cell awake and turned on. No knowing there, but there is knowing that comes after, when we've gotten glimpse of what is possible, of what's beyond, dropping into the mysteries.

The Eleusinian Mysteries were annual initiations, secret and open to all, for the cult of Persephone and Demeter. The only requirements for participation were freedom from "blood guilt" (no murders in your past), and speaking Greek. They were based in the town of Eleusis, the name itself a variant of the noun *eleusis*, which means *arrival*. Here you are. Welcome. They were meant to elevate people above the human sphere. They were meant to launch them divinewards. As Cicero says: "In very truth we have learned from [the Mysteries] the beginnings of life, and have gained the power not only to live happily, but also to die with better hope."

We peer into the abyss, tread into the mystery. It's a temporary death—an end to the limits of the self—and an emergence from it in the form of rebirth, a waking up.

And maybe that's what the ancient farmers were up to building Newgrange, a way of pulling the sun back from darkness, to wake it up and return it to earth, with burning fear of cold and hope for spring. It's long ago, and it's right now. It's earth and sun, and the wheel of the year spins on, like the triskelion on stones and the evergreen wreaths on doors. Mistletoe, the evergreen white-berried vine, which grows off the ground in trees, tangled in their branches, was seen as a link between earth and air, a fertility symbol, athrob with life force, its milky jewel berries full of sticky white juice. So come, kiss. Kiss. It might take you somewhere. As the Sibyl tells Aeneas before his journey to the underworld: "No one / may pass below the secret places of earth before / he plucks the fruit" of the famous golden bough, "as mistletoe in the dead of winter's icy forests / leafs with life on a tree that never gave it birth."

Underworlds, otherworlds, so many passageways on this earth to elsewheres, especially during these weeks of the year. The earth is spinning faster. Something quickens in me, too. I liked the way I felt inside the mound of earth at Newgrange. The way I felt there I have only felt there. Not underworld exactly but touched by—turned into—light and darkness, light and time. Not for long. Ten seconds of my life, likely less. I returned to the surface with the others. Fat sheep made small clouds against green hills, river had sky on it, I couldn't speak for a while. What was there to say?

The year is fading. Light is fading. *Solstice* means sun-stilled. We light candles and raise toasts, we smooch in doorways under strung-up plants, we hang lights along the roofline peaks, give gifts, make wishes, laugh and pray and fear. We bring the light into the earth and try to harness the great forces. It's a wild sort of stilling, a thrashing frenzied sort of stilling, a stopping of time, a de-metering, a holding of the breath as the tension builds, as the dark expands, until it cracks and the light drives in. That's the hope. The far-off tinkling of bells could be the harness of the reindeer or the bells around the neck of a goat. Hoofbeats on the roof, hoofbeats thudding in the warm and living hollow of your chest. Pomegranate, holly branch, birch switch, mistletoe. We'll leaf with life and pass below the secret places of this earth.

In Winter We Get Inside Each Other

THE SLEDDING hill in the town I grew up in was on the grounds of an institution for the criminally insane. Hospital Hill, we called it. Or Mental Mountain. It was a great place to sled.

A huge hill, a sledder's heaven, a real wallomping mound of earth, there at the southern edge of the asylum. Steep, long, with a stretch of flat at the bottom wide enough that your ride could run its course without crashing into the barrier of brush and trees or out into traffic on Route 27 beyond. At the top, asylum to our backs, we took our running starts then flung ourselves, belly-flopping onto our inflated snow tubes, and whished down the hill. Or sometimes sitting upright on the tube and someone behind you, parent or pal, put their hands at your shoulder blades, started running, pushing, building speed, until gravity took over and the hill pulled faster than the push, and the hands disappeared from your back, and you were released, hovering over the snow, cold air in your ears, tang of blood on the tongue from a cracked chapped lip, mittens gripping the handles, the high-pitched purr of rubber on snow, snow that had been packed by ride after ride, it was you and the movement, and it never felt crazy to cry out, there by yourself, going faster and faster, in your own private moment of fear and glee. Is that what made the lunatics yell inside their cells? Some same combination of soaring down a mountainside unstoppable? I'm happy, I'm afraid, I feel too much, I have to let it out. A cracking open in the descent. So we surrender. "This is the Hour of Lead—" writes Emily Dickinson:

> Remembered, if outlived
> As Freezing persons, recollect the Snow—
> First—Chill—then Stupor—then the letting go—

People who freeze to death are often found naked, often enough that there's a phrase for it: paradoxical undressing. At the end stages of hypothermia, after shivering and sleepiness and slurred speech, after confusion, hallucinations, slowed heartbeat, there's a phase when it starts to feel like the skin is burning. One theory holds that contracted muscles tire and relax, releasing a heated flood of blood to the ex-tremities, making it feel like the skin is on fire. Coats, socks, bras, pants, every layer gets shed to make the fire feeling go away.

The walk back up the hill took a while, we'd be panting, warmed, ready to ditch a hat or unzip a coat, and the brick building of the hospital loomed into view near the top, bars on all the windows. The hospital closed in 2003, all the windows boarded up with wood painted red. I can feel right now the hands disappearing from my shoulder blades. And I can hear the sound of the alarm when someone escaped from the hospital. Not the blaring tin of car alarm or wheeeuuu whirl of ambulance or clattering clang of grade-school fire drill. More foghorn, deep and low, a soul-stilling moan, as though the bulk-head door to the basement of Hell was being pried open again and again.

It made for some delicious fear at middle-school sleepovers, hearing the alarm in the night, all of us giddy with fright that some escaped maniac would come tap-tapping on the sliding glass door to skin us alive and fry our eyeballs, wet marbles sizzling, blinded white in the pan. We were young. We didn't know what to be afraid of. Was it horror movie threat of violence and perversion? Was it a latent sense that sanity was something we might lose our hold of, too? Was it simply, still and always, the dark? I lay in the dark with my friends, after we'd all gone quiet, wondering if anyone else was awake, listening to the white noise of breath.

I outlived those nights, and remember them, as I might recollect the snow. One of the snowiest albums I know bows to Dickinson and her hour-of-lead lines. The energy of *The Letting Go*, the 2006 record by Bonnie "Prince" Billy, pseudonym of the shapeshifting

Will Oldham, is that of being in the woods as light fades, some hut somewhere in the distance with a glowing hearth to find, but will you find it, or lose your way in the swirl of snow? On that wintery album, the song "Then the Letting Go" is the wintriest of all, a duet dialogue between Oldham and the snow-wraith-voiced Dawn McCarthy. It begins in innocence.

> There was someone a long time ago
> (Come follow me here and then we'll go)
> Who played with me whenever it snowed

A snow-based companionship brings to mind what Mary Ruefle wrote: "Every time it starts to snow, I would like to have sex . . . with the same person, who also sees the snow and heeds it." Snow as ultimatum, as signal, you and I. Snow changes the world. It changes the light. It changes all the edges. Ruefle's poem closes with union: "When it snows like this I feel the whole world has joined me in isolation and silence." A different sort of joining happens at the end of Oldham's song. His companion returns after a long absence, lays her wet head at his feet, says nothing, and falls asleep. The song ends, brutally:

> In the quiet of the day, well, I laid her low
> (You a fire, me aglow)
> And used her skin as my skin to go out in the snow

In winter, we get inside each other. The erotics of the dark, cold season differ from those of summer—not the flirty sundressed frolic, not sultry August sweat above the lip, not tan lines or sand in shoes or the exuberant spill of peony petals. It's a different sort of smolder now. Quilted, clutching, we wolve for one another, ice on the puddles, orange glow from windows against deepest evening blue. For rare, magnificent moments, we halt time.

In the dark glow, an underblanket musk, it comes from the glands, from deeper inside than in summer, that's how it smells, touch press, it rises, the scent from inside, from between the creases, salt tang and private, and a shift of bodies under the blanket brings it up from below, the inside of the body breathed in. The flinty smell of snowsky outside, and inside, in winter, the body smell is charged, way off at the edges, with fear. I breathe you in, I take you into my blood. In summer: lust and laze, days are loose and lasting. In winter: time tightens, night's wide open, the hunger says *right now*. In winter: the flash of wet light reflected in another's eye, close to yours, half closed in the dim. That eye shining in the dark, that blurred wet glaze and shine, everything else in shadow, form and heat, that light for a flash as lid closes or head shifts, that is a mysterious and singular light. That is the burning animal inside trying to run through the walls of its pen. I see in that flash the burning animal inside you. I feel my own there, too.

It is the animal in us that knows the dark. This season stirs that animal in us, and stirs the memories, ones that live in all of us, submerged so deep, of the ancient dark, of a time before gods, before form and words and light. Memories of helplessness. Somewhere, deep in, we remember. The animal in us remembers. It's those memories, flashing from a great distance, that drive us to string up lights and map the sun and fuck for our lives. Winter reminds us: the dark was first.

I used to think eros was the glowing, driving force behind it all, the heat that propelled all action. But eros is one key into the cave that holds a deeper force.

It is something like this: walk out of the house in the night with your boots on, walk to the well in the snow. Lean over, look in; at a great depth, the black surface of the water reflects a flash of light. Lower the bucket into the well, hear the splash echo up the walls of the well when bucket hits the surface, and feel the resistance on the rope in your hands, the tug of the weight, as water fills it up. The force answers back. You can pull the bucket up now, heavy and full, and drink from it, the water is cold and it tastes like stone. This is the force of eros, an empty bucket dropped into a well to be answered back by the water and brought to your lips to drink.

Or you can keep lowering the bucket, let it drop deeper. Do not pull it up. What's down there? It's so dark. What's down there? Childhood, imagination, all the myths, the monsters and the dragons, ferocious and multiple. This is the force below eros. Eros is the bucket that drops into the well, the desire for water led you there. Eros brought you to the well, and leads you to the place below it. The place below is fearsome, not just for the monsters, but because below *it* is nothing, the icy roar of the void, the ancient dark, when it is your soul against the ice stone. There is nothing there and it ignites our molten human drive for something, something, there cannot be nothing, it's unbearable. Make: noise, a song, love, a joke, a baby, a fire, a friend. What we do, the best of us, our love, our faith, our music, our passion, our stories, all our stories trying to make sense of the chaos, trying to make sense of the fear, come rushing from the deepest place in this well with no bottom to it. Haul that bucket back and drink everything you can from it and walk back to the house in your boots, the crunch of the snow under a winter moon. There is warmth to be had, a hearth, blankets, the glow of a lamp through the glass. Winter tells the secrets of the longer, longest, endless dark and cold that was, and the longer, longest, endless dark to come. Grip tight, press hard. Such is winter love.

I'm putting on another layer. One fantasy I have is skating along a frozen river for miles and miles. It's still possible in Canada, I've heard, and northern Europe. The rivers freeze and one can go and go.

In the town where I grew up, we skated on Kingsbury Pond, across the street from St. Edwards and a tilted old farmhouse. We skated around a small island in the middle of the pond. I always hurried around the far side, briefly out of sight of the parents and the cars, racing along as though being chased up the stairs at night. The shivery risk: the ice might crack, I might fall through, a version of being buried alive, cold dark water and scratched glass sky. The singular creak and groan of ice shifting, it's otherworldly, and frightening, the handsaw twang of bending metal, the ice moaning under the weight of bodies pressed upon it, a deep and dreadful alarm, the ice crying out, *I am about to crack.* I didn't want to fall through there on the far side, into the dark cold water, with no one close to pull me back up to the surface.

"The fountain of youth is ice," writes poet Rebecca Morgan Frank. Cell-stilling ice. Death-defying ice—slow it all down then warm it back to life. Winter is springed. Ice hasn't arrived on the river yet, but it will, and it comes in different colors. Pewter, silver, tarnished metal. One night, I could almost taste it on my tongue, the scratch and tang of the metal at the back of the oven. Up where the river's wide, under the bridge that connects the two cities, it once glowed lavender, pale ghost of flower. Along the Esplanade, under the mist, the ice was aquamarine. Water stilled, the flow solidifies, and one can walk upon a place where one would otherwise fall in.

A good quality of winter, and what a sadness that ice is going extinct. Time-slowing, time-halting ice.

Did you skate as a child, on rivers or ponds? Did you sled? Do you remember the last time you skated? The last time you rode a sled? The fountain of youth is ice, it knives us back and slows us down. Winter invites a turning in, a quieting, an upped interiority. It's dark in there. How deep in the well will you go? Will you be able to find your way out? Time will tell. For now, right now, here we are. An assertion—a reminder—of aliveness. Or as Japanese poet Issa puts it:

> Here,
> I'm here—
> the snow falling.

The snow falling. Here, falling, crystal quiet. It's a quiet that's captured in the documentary *Into Great Silence*, about a Carthusian monastery in the French Alps. The director requested permission to film the monks in 1984. They told him they'd think about it. Sixteen years later they wrote back. *We're ready.* The film, which came out in 2005, is nearly three hours long; there are almost no words. "Our principal endeavor and our vocation is to devote ourselves to the silence and solitude of the cell," states Carthusian Statutes 4.1. The quiet cell, stilled and silent. It returns me to Mary Ruefle's sense when it snows that she's joined by the whole world in isolation and silence. How different, I thought at first. But maybe not. Maybe the union is the same. To take another into oneself, to take the world into oneself, to feel God inside oneself, to feel the whole big show inside oneself, connected, joined, all together. The monks of this monastery devote their time on this earth to silent prayer, there in their cells in the mountains.

The film shows one wrenching, beautiful scene: a group of monks on the mountain, eight of them, white-robed figures ascend a steep and snowy hillside, stony crags above them, camera at a distance, we see human forms but not faces. A meditative stroll, maybe. Get the blood moving in the winter months. But then, look, two monks sit down in the snow, they lift their feet and slide down the sweep of mountain! And then the others, some sitting, some skidding down on their feet, two almost crash into each other, they tumble, they roll down the hill in the snow in their white robes. Down they go! And all one hears is their laughter and their whoops, their joyful noise rising up to heaven. Crying out as they pick up speed, the child in all of us, the hands letting go.

The dark was first, and it will be last. So comes the wordless cry. If you have voice, cry out. In thrashing pleasure, in joy, in heaving grief, in fear. In all of it at once. This is the winter dance, the heated press and spin, between the urgent hunger of the now and the submerged memories of what used to be, the original dark, the first rush down the snowy hill, the skates laced tight around the ankles. Pressing old December dark sweeps its way across the city. It sweeps its way across the river, the forests, the towns with their driveways and church parking lots, the silent ponds, the mountains, the wide flat fields, the hills, the hospitals. It returns us to the wistful hush of the first falling snow and opens a door to a place beyond what we know. The flash of light reflected in the dark water of the well, it could be the moon, it could be the white flame of your very soul.

Burn Something Today

I T'S DARK. I am up early enough to see the stars. The porch light on the house across the street shines bright enough to bring shadows into the room. The neighborhood is still. The rattling newspaper delivery van has not yet been by, the morning news not yet tossed on stoops. Frost not dew, the grass is stiff. A woman scrapes ice off her windshield and I feel it in my teeth. Mothwinged darkness opens itself widest now. Today is the shortest day of the year.

Wasn't it just summer?

Or was summer a thousand years ago?

Was summer?

I place a candle on the windowsill. The flame sways and whips, dancing with the air leaking in from the seams of the old window, writhing against the surface of the predawn blue. The glass brings the orange-white shimmer back into the room.

From the end of the block, headlights beam against the sycamore trunk and light the fences and sidewalk curbs. The newspaper delivery van, a tired russet color with scars of rust on the doors, rattles down the street. It pauses in front of my windows with a moan from the brakes and the delivery man grabs a blue-bagged paper from a heap between the seats and from his open window flings it to the porch across the street. It thuds against the door, the porch light wobbles from the impact. The van moves on, returning the street to its quiet and its darkness, and the facts and stories of the day sit waiting to be brought into the house.

Now it's now. Here we are. The solstices are for fire. Summer flames say *Keep the light alive* (it's never worked, not once). In winter, a more urgent message: *Bring light back to life* (it's worked every time so far). The summer solstice scene is loose and dewy, flower-crowned crowds in debauch around the bonfires, people leaping over flames, and tongues of flame licking up high into the night. In winter: private fire, home hearths.

Soon, my neighbor, a fifty-something psychologist, barefoot in a hooded sweatshirt and pants low on his waist, will open his front door and bend for the paper. He'll stand and cough and the high wheeze will move up and down the block. He'll slam the door and the brass knocker will let one sharp clang. After that, maybe he'll sit at the kitchen table and read the news with coffee steaming from a mug. And maybe this evening, on this longest night, he will crumple the pages in his hands, newsprint on his fingertips dark as ash, making the paper into balls to stuff below the cast-iron grate in his fireplace, laying logs atop, and maybe he will strike a match and hold it to the paper, and maybe he'll sit back on his heels at the hearth as the flames take hold, his face lighting up in the glow as the fire moves across the bed of crumpled newsprint and is drawn up the dark throat of the flue. Crouched on his heels he'll watch as one log catches, and the flames rise higher. And he'll feel the heat on his forehead and across his cheeks and across his shoulders and his chest. And he'll experience a primal satisfaction—I created this warmth—and with this, safe and warm and proud, he'll move to a favorite chair with a book that he'll look up from now and then to see if the fire needs feeding, if it needs another log to eat, to bring warmth and light into this room. To share a room with flame is to feel a living presence in the room with you. As Basho writes:

Fireplace
On the wall
A shadow of the guest

Guest present and guest past, guest seen and unseen. Who do you invite in on the longest night? What visitors arrive? The soul is thicker in winter. Thick enough to cast shadow on the wall.

I don't know what my neighbor will do with his newspaper. Maybe he'll wrap presents with it. Maybe it'll end up in the big blue recycling bin. But maybe it will burn.

The Yule log didn't begin as a cocoa confection with meringue mushrooms on the top. It was oak burned on the night of the solstice. Whole trunks were brought into the home, carried by people with clean hands, and burned night after night during this darkest stretch of the year. A section of the log was saved to light the next year's fire, the strands of light connecting one year to the next. Depending on where one lived, the ashes of the solstice fire were then spread on fields over the following days to up the yield of next season's crops, or fed to cattle to fatten them and boost fertility in the herd, or placed under beds to protect against thunder and lightning, or sometimes worn in a vial around the neck. The lights we string on bushes, that glow on the trees in the center of town—something of these ancient fires lives in them, too. The ancient cults cast shadows in our minds, shift and flicker, their fears are still our fears, down in the darkest places of ourselves.

We're on the edge, teetering toward the other side of something. But what? Winter? It's more than that. An unfamiliar wavelength of darkness and unknown has descended, not for the first time, and maybe not for the last, but it is here. In licoricey unsleeping night, one passes through the daily indignities, frustrations, regrets, and wonders, *Are we going to be okay?* Or, graver and more accurate, *Are we going to survive?* In this way, right now, on this winter solstice, perhaps the glowing strands that connect us to who and what has come before glow brighter now than usual. In this dark season, we are more kindred with the long-gone farmers, lighting their fires, collecting their ash, trying to bring light and warmth back to the land to keep the human scene around, there on their mountainsides, their desert camps, their swamps, hills, prairies, plains, forest glades, wherever they were, under the glittering stars, shivering with cold and the chill of not knowing: will we make it out of this alive?

This what? This season, this darkness, this chaos, this instability, this fire and this cold? As anyone who's balled a fistful of snow barehanded knows, the cold burns, too. "Every child knows that fire and snow are no longer opposites. Not in a radioactive world," writes Inger Christensen. "We're now so fearful that we're not even fearful anymore, but the fear is spreading anyway, and the closest word for it is sorrow."

Fear is spreading because it sells and it sells because it gets at what is animal in us. We buy it and spread it, chaotic and desperate, and it mutates, shifts into something other than it was and, as Christensen says, the closest word for it is sorrow. This is the season we've entered, a season of sorrow, when fire and snow are no longer opposites. This is our radioactive world, our world of fury and confusion, our world of global ailment, of poverty and hunger, of forced migration, our world of information glut, our world where insecure and unhinged leaders stoke fears then bank on them, our world where people's homes are filled with river water or ocean water, mud and seaweed on the countertops, our world where a careless flick of a match turns thousands of acres to ash, where the sun becomes a peach-colored eye through the smoke, our world where the bugs are dying and the birds. It is not new, this shared sense of end, and that is some comfort, surely. But the sense exists regardless: we are in our darkest hour.

My candle burns in the windowsill. Dawn has not dissolved the stars. In this small city where I am, today, the shortest day, light lives for nine hours, four minutes, twenty-nine seconds. Tomorrow, darkness begins to exhale. One two three seconds more of daylight. We won't see it. It's not perceptible, not yet. In time, the seconds accumulate, the light accumulates, and some unexpected evening next month, you might look around and see a different quality of light at almost five. The same way you might, in the thick of July, notice your evening arriving a little earlier. By February, there's no denying. And in March the light floods in as though a dam has been released. A Chinese folk song marks out the "nines of winter," the nine sets of nine days that begin at the winter solstice. In the first and second nine, don't take your hands out of your pockets; in the third and fourth, you can walk on ice; in the fifth and sixth, willows at the river's edge start to bud; in the seventh, the river opens; in the eighth, swallows return; in the ninth, the oxen are back in the fields. A countdown to make it manageable, it helps to know what to expect. What would the first nine be here? Fire in the sunsets maybe. *I know the days are short,* the sunsets now seem to say, *but here, this fuchsia, this gold, this flame, they're the best I know how to make, take what consolation you can.* Winter is only just beginning, the season starts today, but it carries with it in its large felt sack the return of the sun. Winter begins, and the wheel spins itself toward light.

And I'm spun backwards. Nighttime at the end of a suburban cul-de-sac and the living room is lit by the gold-white lights strung around our Christmas tree to the left of the fireplace by the bay window. I am ten, or eleven or nine, I don't know, and I sit on the blue sofa in the dim and magic light. I've taken an ornament off the tree, a little girl in a woolen hat and a soft red coat riding a toboggan. Where's the rest of my family? Baby brother in his crib, the rest watching TV elsewhere maybe. I sit with this ornament in the palm of my hand and imagine the little girl swooping around on her toboggan, coming to life in the nights after we're all asleep in our beds. She rides with the other ornaments, they all come to life, the wooden lamb with the red wool ribbon around its neck, the tiny ice skaters, the nutcracker with its moveable mouth, the white rocking horse, the dove in its nest, the Santa with his fleet of tiny wooden reindeer, the Santa with his cotton-ball beard, the mouse dressed as a chimney sweep, the silver balls were moonstars. I stand from the couch and zoom the girl on her toboggan as one would a toy airplane. I fly her toward the Christmas tree and glide her up and down around it to summon her friends and bring them to life, come join the night parade. The lights glitter. It's dim in the room and dark outside and it is magic, bright-dark magic. A private charge of being let in on the secret, of being granted entry into a world that's with us that we can't see, I felt the spirit of every ornament alive, the spirit of the tree alive, my own self alive, and everything charged with wish and potential.

I was a child then.

And when I think about this memory, it cracks my heart with an ache I can barely stand.

Why is it? It's not what happens when I think about a childhood visit to the beach, or watching fireworks, or playing outside with my brothers after dinner in the yard. What is it about memories of this time of year that bring this ache? In summer, the warmth and the light, they grease the gears and oil the hinges. It's light till nine o'clock? I have all the time in the world! That is the feel in summer, and that is the feel of childhood: I have time.

It's different in winter.

We're pulled back to childhood and, with the dark and cold, we experience our distance from it, and with that comes the knowing, too, that time is running out. Time gone and time left—winter delivers us this knowledge and with it comes the ache. The knowing rises from these shadows, from the layers of memory and understanding, from the tiny private fire out into the burning core of the stars. The memory of the ancient dark, the memory of your small self on a snow day, the lights in the neighborhood, the scent of pine needle or cinnamon, the wishes and disappointment, the loneliness of childhood. Winter holds it all in its cupped hands. And with it, the understanding, frank and cold, that you and the ones you love, all, at some point, end. The dark makes us see it. And this knowing, however deep in it lives, at whatever barely detectable frequency it hums, is what lights the holy spark in us.

These long nights bring a fire behind my eyes that allows me to see what I cannot see in August or in May. It allows me to see the invisible world. It allows me to see the holy spark behind other people's eyes. It can be frightening and hard to manage, a different wavelength of intimacy and connection, to see into the dark well of someone and see the white flash of their soul, but I love this fire. "Though in many of its aspects this visible world seems formed in love," writes Herman Melville in *Moby-Dick*, "the invisible spheres were formed in fright." What we can see is born of love, what we cannot is born of fear. I'm not sure it's true. I look at the flame on my windowsill. Visible, swaying on the candlewick. Invisible, the warmth, the burning heat that glows unseen. We stand in the dark with strands of light between us. Feel the warmth, the heat, the glow, it's ours to know. I want to give it name and say it to you, but I don't know the words. The soul doesn't let us know, not all the way. We flail and give name to simpler needs. Come. Come closer. Here, sit. Get warm. Do you want honey in your tea? We'll share an orange.

The tip of the wick glows orange and curls to black. To watch a flame is to see something inside happening on the outside. The fire makes visible the force we feel in ourselves, and it makes visible the force in the silent sweeping stars above us. Gaston Bachelard writes of "intimate cosmicity," and of uniting "the outside cosmos with an inside cosmos." There is the math that guides the path of our sun and our path around it, the laws of physics, the magnetic pull of a star that weighs 333,000 times more than this earth. We know that light blasts along at 671 million miles per hour. We know the angle of the axis on which our earth spins, we know the core of the sun burns at twenty-seven million degrees Fahrenheit, we know our life would not exist without it, we need its return, and it will return. We know so much. There are so many facts. And right alongside them, a whole world we can't explain or comprehend, which we cannot give words to, an understanding of presence and goneness, of departure and return, the haunt and mystery, we see it and sense it but cannot say it. And this is the magic, the incomprehensible unsaid, this is the beauty in this dark moment of the year, what we see without seeing. The ornaments coming alive, the ghosts who dug a tunnel under the earth for the sun to enter on the solstice, the silent moon, the snow-white swans, the glittering stars, the twinkling lights on the trees and in the windowsills, behind the eyes of the people we love. This is the magic that glows, that lives alongside the facts, that burns and lights the dark. This dark season, as light presses its way back to us, offers it to us.

On a bridge across the river, a bit of graffiti in small neat letters reads: *look at it all, it is all end full.* All of it, look. All of it, ending. Every moment and everything held in every moment, all of it holding its end. The river and the coats and the fruits with all their colors. The bookcases and the blankets and the branches on the trees. Shoulders, a cardinal, the moon. Look at it all. The brothy golden glow of the kitchen in winter with a soup on the stove. Every embrace. Every spoon. The fire and the frost. It is all end full. Everything that hurts and everything that makes our hearts soar. The gap in the floorboards, the back of a grandmother's hand, the smell of your friend's mother's car, the crumbs on the backseat. The evenings, the mornings, the weather, all the shifting weather. Look at it all. All the hellos and see you soons, brothers laughing. The quiet empty rooms, the last stop, a drink of water before bed. The special warmth between your legs, the riddles, the mud at the riverbank. The boots and the hooves, a flock of sheep on a hill. A clam shell, a vertebra, a church bell. Look at it all. A red scarf, a favorite mug, the eyes of a stranger on the sidewalk. Wind across a sand dune, an icicle off the gutter, your mother's voice saying *goodnight*. It is all end full. The oceans and the shovels and the milk. Ladders, glass, ambulances. Dice in the palm, confusion, your tongue in your mouth. The naked press with another body, wanting, baths, bridges, feathers, fear and love and all the different kinds of light. In the light of the dark look at it all. It is all end full.

AFTERWORD

The Timing of the Light

ON DECEMBER evenings before dinner as kids, my brothers and I went room to room and lit the candles in the windowsills. They were the electric kind, with flame-shaped bulbs on top of plastic candlesticks. Sometimes I stood at the window in my parents' bedroom on the second floor and waited for a car to come, and as it neared the house, I rolled the ridged wheel of the switch to light the candle so that someone in the car might see the light come on, and in that, feel delivered good luck or cheer, a flashing sense of human presence behind the glass. I'm here and you're here and—blink—here's a light for you on your way, on whatever here-to-there you're on, picking your son up at a friend's house, coming home with a load of groceries in the trunk, weary after an afternoon of deadening conference calls. I did not know about conference calls in middle school, but sensed adulthood could be possessed of certain drear. And maybe someone my age was riding in the front seat and saw the light turn on, and felt the warm jolt of magic, like seeing a fox in the snow, or a shooting star, happenstances of reality in this world—foxes exist, space matter tears across the sky, lights turn on—that carry with them meaning beyond the raw fact of the occurrence. A secret bit of fortune, a signal when you needed it, connection to the larger spark. I timed the light with the hope that someone might feel that they were being offered something, because they were.

We're alive which means we won't be and these wordless offerings are an acknowledgement of that fact. It is the season of gifts. A bottle of something handed over as a scarf is unwrapped from the throat. A paper plate with a low pyramid of brownies under foil. A pair of socks with stripes, a cylinder of waxy cherry-flavored chapstick, a subscription to mail order beans. What can I give you? What can any of us give to each other?

I know the feeling in my body when I am all the way here, when I am offering what light I have to you, the most precious thing I have, my attention, which is to say, my love. And I know the feeling in my body when it is returned, when that presence is offered back, when the spark of you is right here with me, even for a moment. It is not the words that speak the presence but the glow behind the eyes, the pulse from the heart communicated between us, across a table, beside you as we walk together on the sidewalk toward the square. I'm here, you're here. We will not always be.

The body registers it because what hums in the background of that presence is absence; around that blaze of light, big darkness roars. Winter tells us, more than petaled spring, or hot-grassed summer, or fall with its yellow leaves, that we are mortal. In the frankness of its cold, in the mystery of its deep-blue dark, the place in us that knows of death is tickled, focused, stoked. The angels sing on the doorknobs and others sing from the abyss. The sun has been in retreat since June, and the heat inside glows brighter in proportion to its absence. We make up for the lost light in the spark that burns inside us.

Maybe it's why I like winter, more than anything the stretch leading up to it. To feel in better, realer touch with strength and fragility, my own and yours. The temporary heat of our aliveness burning at its hottest.

As kids, lighting those candles in the windowsills, we sensed the sanctity of it, the thrilling solemnity, that this was a hallowed act. So much so that we shouldered each other out of the way, jostling to be the one to light a light. Lighting those candles in the prewinter dim was a sacrament untethered to any church or scripture. It did not involve language or any organized notion of god. It was sacred the way sharing a plate of scrambled eggs can be sacred or raising a glass in toast or walking beside someone you love on a path in the woods.

I went to bed those nights leading into winter and the candle brought its tender glow into my bedroom, and I sensed a magic I wasn't sure if I should believe in anymore, that I feared I should've outgrown. I knew I shouldn't speak it outloud, and I'm not sure I would've been able to anyway. So much magic is axed out of us, by the accumulating hurts of adulthood, our imaginations muffled by fear and loss, by the dull chores and arguments that separate us from the type of light and darkness that lives within us and outside us.

The glow in the window was specific to winter, specific to the days leading up to the darkest day of the year. That candle on a night in July would not make available the same charged and powerful hush. We don't need such light in July. We need it in December when the dark darkens the dark. It was not just what the light brought inward to my bedroom, but what it pushed outward, out to the cars on the road and the night travelers, out over the stone walls and the fields and the deer in the moonlight in the quiet backyards where they left hoofprints in the snow, out and up to the stars. I rode out there with it, carried out and out on that fake flame. I can't explain it. There's a belief that's not shamed away on the playground, a faith in something powerful that's communicated across time and space, the strands of light lit up between us. The gift, the miracle of this time of year, it's not that the sun returns nor the barnyard birth of a prophet. It is simpler and more right here.

Snow whispers against the window. It begins to collect on the sidewalks and on the branches of the trees, on the needles of the white pine, on the storm-blue berries of the juniper. The sky is pale. The dark is out there everywhere. Fleets of delivery trucks drop packages on front doorsteps. A present. Here's a present. Here you are, a present, this one, right now, for now. It is for you, for now. All night the snow will fall, the radiator's rasp and clang brings heat into the room, the kettle, quiet, waits to be warmed on the stove, to exhale, in a cloud of steam, its high whistle, urgent and bright.

Plant Matter

The following are the plants and herbs most strongly associated with the winter solstice. They're woven into wreaths, decked in halls, hung on doors and in doorways, draped around banisters, slung on mantles, cooked with, made into tinctures and teas, and burned in fires. Besides the below, other plants and herbs with strong links to the winter solstice include: cedar, clove, rosemary, nutmeg, birch, pine, chamomile, juniper, frankincense, and wintergreen.

Holly

Two brothers run the year, two kings, and each one rules for six months. The cheery Holly King, mischievous in the gloried dark, puts on the crown on the summer solstice and lords over the darkening half of the year. On the winter solstice, at the peak of his power, darkness at its very darkest, daylight at its leanest, he surrenders to the Oak King, who'll have the throne as the sun returns itself to earth. And so they make their solstice trades, power handed back and forth as the seasons swap and the years spin round. The waxy prickled evergreening holly leaves and its firm red balls give a cheering lifeblood impression in winter, a blast of bright color in the dun, and a threatening sense as well, puncturing and poison, vaguely cactal. Evil spirits feared the holly, and people brought it into the house to protect against them. It was said to forfend against lightning, too, and planted near houses because of it. It eats the light, swallows it right down, and drops it to the earth.

Blessed Thistle

The yellow flower has a dandelion look, a sunburst accumulation of tiny petals. It sprawls itself across the earth and needs full sun to grow. A silky white down furs its leaves. It's known also as the holy thistle or the spotted thistle or *Cnicus benedictus* or Saint Benedict Thistle, after Saint Benedict, patron saint of speleologists, people who study or spend time in caves. A full-sun flower, a namesake saint of dark places. Blessed maybe for its healing powers: it can help diarrhea, swelling, and coughs. It aids in liver function. It can lower fevers and treat bacterial infections. Blessed maybe for the Benedictine monks who used it to soothe the fester and puss of bubonic wounds during the plague. Monks turned it into tonic and chugged it.

It's also used as a galactagogue, increasing breast milk supply for nursing mothers, making a milkier way.

Mistletoe

Mistletoe, a parasitic plant, thieves water and nutrients from its host, often an oak. A bird eats the white berry, shits a seed upon a tree, the seed embeds itself into the tree's system, a significant kiss, slipping into its xylem, the place where the mistletoe takes what it needs to grow. In Norse myth, Balder, beloved god of light and joy and the summer sun, son of goddess Frigg and god Odin, had bad dreams about his death. To protect him, his mom made every creature and every object vow never to bring him harm. Everything and everyone agreed. Except mistletoe, which Frigg had never asked. Loki, the disruptor, learned this and made a spear of the mistletoe and joined a game the gods liked to play where they'd shoot arrows and throw things at Balder; every hurled weapon missed its mark. Loki in disguise handed the spear made of mistletoe to Balder's blind twin brother, the winter god, telling him to toss it. He did, the spear reached its target, and Balder fell down dead. Goodnight warmth, goodnight sun. In the underworld, goddess Hel said he'd be released only if everything in the world would weep for him. Everything did, except Loki in disguise again, and so Balder remained. Some say Frigg's tears turned into the white berries of the mistletoe and that they brought him back to life. And so the mistletoe became a symbol of love, kisses all around. Other versions aren't so tidy. The Greeks called it Oak Sperm.

Cinnamon

It comes from the innards of the tree, extracted from below the bark and let to dry, and it curls into rolls as it does. Scrolls of rust-colored spice, grated into powder, dusted over the apple crisp, a glass of thick rich eggnog, buttered toast, sugar cookies. A familial smell, a smell that lives in our minds before we've even smelled it, inherited from thousands of years of global trade, of boats and caravans, travelers crossing sea and land to deliver new flavors to the mouth. Cinnamaldehyde brings the smell, an unappealing set of syllables for a smell of warmth, ovens and forests, color of fallen oak leaves, of darkened honey. It's an antioxidant, an anti-inflammatory, it lowers blood sugar. It's said to increase circulation, too, widening the vessels, especially in the abdomen and between the legs. More blood flow, more warmth, a special heat, more babies are conceived this time of year than any other. Rattle of cinnamon stick in the jar, dust on your fingertips, a stranger at the door.

Yew

Aged sentinel of the churchyard, scabby-barked and evergreen, the yew, with its "vast circumference and gloom profound" grows "too slowly ever to decay," as Wordsworth told. The trunk crumbles on the inside, and as it does, aerial roots, roots from above, drop into the crumbled hollows and down into the ground, new life in dead space. You cannot tell the age of the yew tree, not in the usual way—no age rings there to count. Their lifespan is tallied not in decades but millennia, and they were associated with the underworld, said to hold life and death not in opposition but twined like light and dark. "Beneath the shadows cast by somber yews, / there is a path that, sloping downward, moves / through voiceless silences—the road that leads / to the infernal world, where sluggish Styx / exhales its fog and mists," writes Ovid in his *Metamorphoses*. They cleansed souls on their way to the underworld. The dead are outside time, and as for plant life on this earth, the yew might get closest to that same sort of spanlessness. Because of this, they're often found by graveyards, roots tickling the dreamless skulls. The bark is the source of paclitaxel, known as Taxol, an anticancer compound that helps halt cell splitting in cancers of the ovary, lung, breast, and esophagus, among other sites of solid tumors. How still the graveyard, how still the church, how still the mossy stones, and the yew tree, quietly, so quietly, grows into its own hollows. You can't hear it happening, but it's happening, new roots growing to fill the voids. And the thrushes and the waxwings come to gulp the berries, the fleshy, gummy cases of the poisonous seeds.

Oak

What's fire's relationship to the sky? Does fire eat sky? Does sky eat the fire? Does the sky burn, feel hurt, cry out, as flames rip into it, as the oak in the fire moves from tree bone to tree dust, silky black ash back to earth? Or does the sky say to the fire, Yes, take me in, turn me to heat, turn me to light, make me disappear? Does the fire say to the sky, Closer, let me touch you? Does the sky say, Fire, dance in me, lick me? Does fire say, Sky, increase me, let me fill you all the way? Does the sky say, Fire, you know when you feel the wind that we are moving together in the ancient way? Is the fire afraid of what will happen? What will happen? The fire will rise, swell, flick, lick, throw shadows on the snow, bring blood to the foreheads, cheeks, and necks of the ones who stand near it. It will feast on the oak, ravenous fire, it will eat the oak, the oak in its potency, its longevity, king tree, door to another world. Fire will feed on tree, and once it's taken what it can from it, and taken what it can from the sky, the glow will grow lower, like a dancer who's danced for days, danced holes into shoes, and faded on the floor. Then, oak eaten, only glow on the ground, the embers will throb with orange heat. And the sky will take the last gray-white strand of smoke into itself and spread it so thin it turns into smell, on the shoulders of the people near the fire, in their hair, in the fur that lines the hoods of their coats, in the fur of the fox that hid nearby to watch the flames because it's the closest the fox gets to looking in the mirror. That last wisp will rise into the night as the eyelid falls over the glow, blinking it to black ash. But an end here does not mean the end. The original fire lives in all fire. On the stove and in the hearth, in the bonfire on the beach, surrounded by stones in the woods by a river, in the explosion after the crash, between your ribs and behind your eyes, on the struck tip of the match, on the burning surface of the stars, the source of our fire, and us all. The fire goes out and lives on. The burnt dust of oak bone will rise, like you someday, and me, like all of us, last branches turned to ash, last branches of the great tree that rooted us, everything, all together, up to where the sky becomes something else, a place that doesn't belong to us, and that tiny speck of tree will continue to rise, invisible, barely there, up and up, until up no longer exists, until it's drawn into the path of the galloping golden horses that pull the sun.

Works Cited

Gaston Bachelard, *The Poetics of Reverie: Childhood, Language, and the Cosmos*, translated by Daniel Russell (Presses Universitaires de France, 1960 / Beacon, 1969).

Matsuo Basho, *The Essential Haiku: Versions of Basho, Buson & Issa*, translated and edited by Robert Hass (Ecco, 1995).

Bonnie "Prince" Billy, "Then the Letting Go," from *The Letting Go* (Drag City, 2006).

Henri Bosco, *Malicroix*, translated by Joyce Zonana (Éditions Gallimard, 1948 / NYRB, 2020).

Inger Christensen, *The Condition of Secrecy*, translated by Susanna Nied (Glydendal, 1964 / New Directions, 2018).

Cicero, *On the Republic. On the Laws*, translated by Clinton Keyes (Loeb Classical Library, Harvard University, 1928).

Emily Dickinson, "After a great pain, a formal feeling comes — (341)" from *Final Harvest: Emily Dickinson's Poems* (Little, Brown, 1961).

Rebecca Morgan Frank, "I hold with those who favor fire" from *Oh You Robot Saints!* (University of Chicago, 2021).

Philip Gröning, dir. *Into Great Silence* (Zeitgeist Films, 2005).

Kerry Howley, *Thrown* (Sarabande, 2014).

Kobayashi Issa, *The Essential Haiku: Versions of Basho, Buson & Issa*, translated and edited by Robert Hass (Ecco, 1995).

Han Kang, *The White Book*, translated by Deborah Smith (Munhak Dongne, 2016 / Hogarth, 2019).

Herman Melville, *Moby-Dick or The Whale* (Penguin Classics, 1992).

Ovid, *The Metamorphoses of Ovid*, translated by Allen Mandelbaum (Harvest, 1993).

Octavio Paz, *The Labyrinth of Solitude*, translated by Lysander Kemp (Grove, 1961).

Mary Ruefle, "Snow" from *The Most of It* (Wave, 2008).

Virgil, *The Aeneid*, translated by Robert Fagles (Penguin, 2006).

William Wordsworth, "Yew-Trees" from *Selected Poems* (Penguin Classics, 2005).

Acknowledgments

Thank you to Nadja Spiegelman who originally assigned these essays for the *Paris Review.* Thank you to Joshua Bodwell, Celia Blue Johnson, and Beth Blachman at Black Sparrow, and thank you to my agent Gillian MacKenzie. Thank you to Will Oldham for the use of his lyrics and for the pleasure his music has given me. Thank you to Michael Russem. Thank you to the Charles River and Walden Pond. Thank you to Will and Sam and my parents and Pam. Thank you to Alicia Simoni, Éireann Lorsung, John Daniels, Sharon Steel, Lisa Gozashti, Jenny Kuliesis, Jonah Fontela, and especially to Kim Adrian.

Printed August 2023 in Hanover, Pennsylvania for the Black Sparrow Press by Sheridan. Text set in Bembo with Mrs. Eaves for titling. Interior design by Brooke Koven. Cover design by Jennifer Muller. Composition by Tammy Ackerman. This first edition has been bound in paper wrappers.

Black Sparrow Press was founded by John and Barbara Martin in 1966 and continued by them until 2002. The iconic sparrow logo was drawn by Barbara Martin.